LET'S TALK ABOUT

DISOBEYING

REVISED FOR EDUCATIONAL USE

By Joy Wilt Berry
Illustrated by John Costanza

 CHILDRENS PRESS ™

CHICAGO

Let's talk about DISOBEYING.

When you do not do
what you are asked to do,
you are DISOBEYING.

Your parents,
your teachers,
or other adults who care for you,
have good reasons
for telling you what to do
or what not to do.

Caring adults
tell you what to do,
or what not to do,
because they do not want you
to hurt yourself
or others.

Caring adults
tell you what to do,
or what not to do,
because they do not want you
to ruin your things
or other people's things.

9

Caring adults
tell you what to do,
or what not to do,
because they want you
to be liked
by other people.

Caring adults
tell you what to do,
or what not to do,
because they want you
to be fair.

13

Caring adults
tell you what to do,
or what not to do,
because they love you
and they care about
the people around you.

But still,
you may have questions:

Why do they get to
tell me what to do?

Why can't I
decide for myself?

Adults have lived
much longer than you have,
so they have learned more.

Because they know more,
they usually know
what is best for you.

The adults who care for you
are *responsible* for you
and for your actions.

If you do something
to hurt yourself
or others,
they may have
to take care of any damage.

If you disobey them,
they may have to punish you.

They hope the punishment
will help you to remember
not to disobey again.

If you are punished,
   you will feel bad,
   you will be sorry, and
   you will not want to disobey again.

21

If you do not want
to be punished,
it might help to:

Find out what people want you to do
and what they do not want you to do.

Listen to the adults who care for you.
Be sure you understand
what they are saying.

Ask questions
if you are not sure what they mean.

You may not agree with
the adults who care for you.

But do not nag
or throw a tantrum.

Try to tell them how you feel.

They may change their minds.

If they do not,
don't talk about it anymore.

That will only upset you,
and it may make them angry.

Once you understand what they want,
do what they want you to do.

If you do disobey,
don't lie about it.

Lying will only
make things worse.

If you do disobey:

Tell the truth.

Say you are sorry
and mean it.

Accept your punishment.

Don't be angry.
Remember, it was you
who disobeyed.

Try not to disobey again.

When you obey,
you will please
those who care for you
and you will be doing
what is best for yourself.

About the Author
Joy Berry is the author of more than 150 self-help books for
children. She has advanced degrees and credentials in both
education and human development and specializes in working with
children from birth to twelve years of age. Joy is the founder of the
Institute of Living Skills. She is the mother of a son, Christopher,
and a daughter, Lisa.